AF441875

Contents

Introduction

Have you ever felt another person's soothing energy? It might feel warm, nurturing, and incredibly healing. And have you ever felt that same energy inside yourself, in moments of peace or during yoga practice when you can feel your own life force swirling within you. Reiki is a little like that. It's a form of energy healing that dates back to the late 19 Century, yet its benefits can easily apply to the modern world. Here's what to know about this gentle practice.

Reiki is a form of alternative therapy commonly referred to as energy healing. It emerged in Japan in the late 1800's and is said to involve the transfer of universal energy from the practitioner's palms to their patient. Energy healing has been used for centuries in various forms. Advocates say it works with the energy fields around the body. Some controversy surrounds Reiki, because it is hard to prove its effectiveness through scientific means. However, many people who receive Reiki say it works, and its popularity is increasing. A Google search for the term currently returns no less than

68,900,000 results. A 2007 survey shows that, in the United States (U.S.), 1.2 million adults tried Reiki or a similar therapy at least once in the previous year. Over 60 hospitals are believed to offer Reiki services to patients.

Although there are many forms of energy healing in cultures throughout the world, the specific practice of Reiki was developed in the late 1800s by a Buddhist monk turned Japanese doctor named Dr. Mikao Usui. While meditating for 21 days, he discovered the ability to heal through gentle touch or near touch. Later, one of Dr. Usui's pupils, Dr. Chujiro Hayashi continued and expanded the practice, including many of the hand positions used today. Reiki is rooted in the philosophy that one person's transfer of energy can stimulate healing energy in another. It's based on the idea that an unseen universal life-force energy flows through us, licensed massage therapist and Reiki master, and author of Y. "In yoga, we call it prana; the Japanese call it ki. Today, the International Center for Reiki Training estimates that more than 4 million people have studied Reiki, and more than 800 American hospitals incorporate it as a way to help patients manage pain.

Reiki

Reiki is a form of energy healing that involves light (or no) touch. Using gentle hand movements, Reiki practitioners guide energy within a person's body to encourage self-healing, according to the National Center for Complementary and Integrative Health (NCCIH). While there is still little conclusive evidence to explain precisely how or why Reiki works, there is a growing body of data suggesting it helps some people with sleep, pain, anxiety and depression, stress management, and symptom management for chronic health problems.

One theory behind Reiki is that interactions between the energy field (also known as the "biofield") of the practitioner and the energy field of the recipient trigger the healing effects,

Reiki gently encourages the person's system to restore balance, a New York City–based Reiki master and researcher who has collaborated with the medical schools at Harvard and Yale to help develop Reiki programs there.

Primarily, Reiki shifts your body's stress response from its "fight-or-flight" state to a more restful state during and immediately after the session, which is better for your well-being and your health in the long run. (Being in fight-or-flight mode triggers the release of stress hormones and other physiological changes that can be damaging if experienced constantly.) Then, once your body is less stressed, it can better heal itself

Reiki is a method of working with spiritual energy. Sometimes, this energy is called Reiki, but it is misleading, as the energy itself does not have name, only the method can be called Reiki. But, we used to say that "I channel Reiki", and this is correct. Because this way, we know what kind of energy we're working with. The word Reiki itself can be translated as "universal spiritual energy".

Reiki is a system, to which you need to be initiated. You can become self-attuned, but remember, that Mikao

Usui, the creator of the system, lived in XIX/XX-century Japan, and he was a Buddhist. And that he spend give or take 20 years until he achieved his Satori, and learned Reiki on his own. Initiation, so called attunement, is much faster way of becoming a Reiki practitioner.

You may find a lot of self-attunement CD's and books and instructions. Please, do not be mislead. 99.9% people living modern lives in modern civilization cannot attune themselves. They need someone else to attune them, really. But it's worth it, definitely.

The Short History Of Reiki
Reiki was re-discovered by Mikao Usui (1864-1926), in Japan, at the beginning of the XX century. Usui was a Buddhist practitioner, and after 21 days of meditation on Mount Kurama (or Kuri Yama), he self-attuned himself to Reiki energy, and he begin sharing his knowledge with others. His knowledge was passed to hundreds if not thousands of people, and few dozens of Reiki teachers. One of these teachers, Hayashi, passed his knowledge to Takata, and she brought Reiki to United States.

From United States, Reiki expanded into almost every corner of the world, and today, it's very easy to find a Reiki teacher that can initiate you into this practice. Of course, this is a very short version of Reiki history, but basically, that's all that you need to know. Reiki is a system that originates from Qigong and Buddhist practices, and it has something in common with Shinto religion, too. But you don't need to be a Buddhist to become a Reiki practitioner.

As for the energy itself, it existed from the very beginning. And it was often used in Buddhist medicine practices, in Taoist practices, in Qigong, and in other parts of the world. The names are different, but the energy is the same.

There is a version of Reiki history that says Usui was a Christian priest on Christian university in Japan. And that he studies in United States and that he traveled all across the world, searching for his Satori. This story is not true. It was, probably, made up by Takata, in order to persuade Americans to Reiki. Takata brought Reiki to

USA after the 2nd World War, so you can imagine how could people react for the Japan healing method.

What Is Reiki Initiation

Reiki is a universal energy. It doesn't matter who you are, what do you believe in etc. If you wish to become a Reiki practitioner, all you have to do is to find a teacher that will give you attunements. You may find a teacher that is willing to initiate you for free, but most of the time, it costs money. There must be this energy exchange going on and giving something money in exchange for a service, is an energy exchange.

Reiki initiation, or attunement, is quite simple. The teacher expands your energetic channels (called Meridians in China, or Nadi in India, or just energy channels), and prepares your chakras for channeling Reiki. Each initiation takes up to 20, maximum 30 minutes. So it's not long. Oh, and during initiation, you can keep your clothes on, you don't need to pray to any entity or deity, there are no additional attributes. You just sit, relax, and the teacher initiates you. So, it's very normal, very safe, and not very extraordinary.

Rates vary from teacher to teacher. You can become initiated for $100, for $250 if it's first degree, similar price applies to second degree, and third degree's price can be anything from $400 to $2000.

I recommend individual courses, because this way, you can ask more questions to your teacher, and get more detailed answers. A course takes from one to two days, yet some teachers expand it for a whole week, too. And of course, your attunement should take place face-to-face. Most advanced Reiki teachers agree, that distant attunements are not full attunements, and they're just a waste of money. Therefore, distant initiation is not recommended.

During my own initiation, there were no fireworks, no deities, no spirits. Actually, I felt quite relaxed and nicely grounded. Yet I've heard stories of teachers who initiate in the name of Jesus Christ. Well, remember that Reiki is not connected to any religion. It's a technique that uses universal spiritual energy. It can be associated with Holy Spirit, or Chi, or God, but it's energy, and it's a method. It's not related to any religion.

Three Degrees

I've mentioned that there are three degrees in Reiki practice. First, Second, Third (some teachers divide the third degree into 3a and 3b, first for 3rd degree, second type for teacher training). Now, let's discuss these degrees a bit.

First degree is meant to introduce you to Reiki energy, and start your physical healing process. From first degree on, you can channel Reiki to others, and perform this form of psychic healing. You can give Reiki to food, objects, plants, animals and so on. This is the degree that I recommend to everyone.

Second degree gives you three Reiki signs to work with. They act as additional tools that support your focus, intention and energy flow. Your energy channels are expanded, and Reiki beings your emotional and spiritual cleansing. From now on, you're on the good path of spiritual growth.

Third degree gives you the fourth symbol, sometimes called master symbol, and with enough training, you can initiate others into the practice after the third degree. Third degree is focusing on your spiritual growth, and the fourth sign is meant mainly for your personal meditation and growth.

With each degree, the energy within you flows better, and you channel Reiki easier. It is a gentle process of Reiki development. I do not advise taking all three degrees at once, even if the teacher advises that. Wait 3 months between first and second degree, and wait at least a year between second and third degree. This way, you make sure that you won't be hit hard by the cleansing period.

Reiki flows better with time. From my own practice, I can say there's a huge difference in the energy flow, and your entire life after few months of work. The more you work with Reiki, the more changes you see and the better the energy flows. Therefore, do not be disappointed if nothing extra-ordinary happens after few months after your first degree.

Is Reiki Right for Me

As Reiki is gentle and noninvasive, it's really safe for everyone, says Vickie Bodner, a licensed massage therapist and Reiki master in the Center for Integrative Medicine at Cleveland Clinic in Ohio. People most commonly seek Reiki to help them prepare for or recover from surgery, manage stress and anxiety, cope with the loss of a loved one, or as an adjunct to professional medical care, like cancer treatment, Bodner says. Some people seek Reiki for supportive touch when they feel alone in dealing with troubling situations. Reiki may be especially helpful if you haven't seen results from other treatments or solutions. "If nothing else is working, it's usually because the [nervous] system is so stressed," Miles says. Reiki may boost the effectiveness of other medical treatments by reducing stress, which can be a roadblock.

But Reiki is not a substitute for medical treatment. "People should always contact a doctor for professional help for any medical or mental [health] issues," Bodner says. Once you've gotten help from a professional, Reiki may be added as a form of complementary care.

What Reiki Gives You

Reiki is a healing practice but it heals not just your physical body, but also your mind, your soul, your emotions. It helps you work out your negative mind patterns and core images. What can it gives you? A lot of things, I would say:

It can heal physical illnesses that doctors thought to be impossible to heal. I've heard stories of females being unable to give a birth, yet becoming pregnant after few Reiki sessions.

It can solve problems. If you suffer from family problems, or job problems, or any other kind of problems, Reiki can bring balance. It helps finish the unfinished business, solve life problems, and bring harmony back to your life.

It's a way to develop psychic abilities. With Reiki, you can cleanse your chakras, and remove blockages, and become attuned to your psychic intuition again. And I don't have to remind you that this is a path towards psychic awakening, right?

Reiki can speed up your spiritual growth, because it helps you clear your blockages, and focus on your own spiritual development more. Get rid of negative habits, improve your life, deal with blockages, find your true passion, enjoy life more. This is a path of becoming a better person.

Reiki gives you a way to help others, too. You can channel Reiki to people, animals and plants. To food and electronic devices. To places and events. To past and future. Reiki is an energy that can heal, yes. But this healing is not limited to the physical body. Reiki can heal everything!

And this list is just a short selection of things that Reiki gives you. It can literally change your life for better, if you allow it. If you have more questions about Reiki, ask them in the comments, and I will be happy to answer them.

How it works
Reiki is based on the pre-scientific belief that an unseen 'life force energy (prana) animates the living. When this energy is low, one is more likely to feel sick and unhappy and if it is high, one may feel healthy and happy. Reiki removes blocks to the flow of energy in our body and facilitates balance and support on all levels that can help to cure stress, discomforts and even chronic diseases.

The practitioner places her/his hands on or near a person's body in a series of hand positions. These include positions around the head and shoulders, the stomach, and feet. Then, the transfer of Reiki energy from practitioner to patient takes place to restore and balance natural life force energy within body. When Reiki begins, a person tends to achieve a unique physical and emotional balance. However, it shouldn't be confused with the manipulation of a person's subconscious mind. "Reiki is not related to any type of black magic, hypnotism or psychology, necromancy etc. It has no dogma, and there is nothing you must believe in order to learn and use Reiki.

Willingness is necessary
Even though 'belief' has nothing to do with Reiki, it will work whether or not you believe in it; yet willingness to heal is necessary. When a person's willingness to heal is strong, the results are hard to deny.

It's simple when a person is resistant to the Reiki energy, he will not let the Reiki in. Similarly, a partially receptive person will only receive whatever he is willing to receive. And, such is the case with conventional medicine too; a patient's recovery is often attributed to his attitude and his will to get better.

The miracles
The website of International Center For Reiki Training is loaded with testimonials by people, who are believed to have benefitted immensely by this healing technique. Reiki has shown miraculous results on all forms of illness and negative conditions. Through Reiki, the side effects of regular medical treatments have also been

condensed or eliminated. This includes the negative effects of chemotherapy, postoperative pain and other ailments. Reiki is believed to have also improved the healing rate of patients." She further adds that Reiki has the potential to cure headache, stomach pain, bee sting, cold, flu, tension, anxiety as well as serious illness like heart disease, cancer, etc.

Likewise, various first stage cancer patients have got treated; arthritis patients have shown more mobility; and patients diagnosed with diabetes have also shown marked improvement.

However, there's a catch!

Science is pretty hazy regarding the efficacy of Reiki and there are no substantial studies to back up this therapy. Perhaps, this is the reason Reiki has failed to garner mainstream attention in comparison to other alternate therapies such as acupuncture.

Patients, particularly, suffering from cancer should not be deprived of the more effective treatments that the conventional medical care offers. "Simply administering a placebo like Reiki would deprive patients of the specific treatment effect. The allegedly caring approach of some enthusiasts of alternative medicine would therefore rob patients of benefits that they need and deserve.

Switch off, Tune out

People should step off the hedonistic treadmill and think about what really makes them happy. The 'quarter life crisis' generation, running against time, is already fatigued. Does it really matter if one doesn't get that coveted invite to the 'It' party' in town, didn't make an ultra-chic fashion statement, or had that exotic dish in that trendy restaurant? .We are all over-worked, over-fed, over-exhausted and suffer from social media fatigue. Missing out may be the only way to step into the life that actually gives us happiness.

Christina Crook, author of Joy of Missing Out, went on an internet fast – she gave up social media for 31 days to experience a fuller life. At the end of the fast, she experienced emotions that are hard to come by these days – relief and joy. She felt closer to people around her, developed new habits, like writing poetry. Following the herd blindly never results in satisfaction. We find joy and meaning in intentionally choosing our path, and walking forward confidently. If we are choosing to go online because we are motivated by the fear of missing out, we will never be able to stop. But how does one understand what to opt out of at a time when one is sinking into everyday rapids parties, friends, eating out, social media posts etc. with no life-jacket on? Greg McKeown, author of Essentialism, says edit your life as you would edit your wardrobe. "We need to be selective. If it's not a definite 'yes', it's a 'no'."

The Danes know best
One of the key spirits of the Danish culture is 'hygge' (coziness). It refers to creating a warm atmosphere and enjoying the good things in life with good people. Hygge also means making ordinary, everyday things more beautiful or meaningful. Missing out enables you to take control of your wellbeing. It makes an active statement to the world that you are self contained. In the past, our wellbeing was managed by boundaries set by societal

norms. We had delineated weekends and set work hours that ended at 5-or-6 pm. The challenge now is to set your own boundaries. The haves and have-nots of happiness are going to be defined by those who can set their own boundaries, and are capable of saying 'no' to external stimulus.

How Do You Find a Reiki Practitioner

Reiki isn't regulated like other treatment modalities, which means you have to be an informed consumer when it comes to finding a practitioner..

Start by looking at the practitioner's level of training and experience. A well-trained Reiki practitioner should be certified and have received their training in person with a Reiki master teacher who's certified or licensed by a reputable Reiki training organization.

Two large, reputable Reiki training organizations in the United States include the International Center for Reiki Training (ICRT) and the Reiki Alliance. Both have online directories to help you find trained practitioners in your area. The Center for Reiki Research includes a directory of hospitals, medical clinics, and hospice programs where Reiki is offered.

Should You Become Reiki Practitioner
Definitely yes! In my opinion, everyone should receive attunement to first degree, at least. Second and third degree are paths for more advanced spiritual growth, but first degree is meant for you, and those close to you. You can heal yourself, and heal others, and begin your life anew with, or without spirituality. Some things may change, and some things may remain the same, but growth is the reason why we are here.

There is an argument among certain people, that they wish not to try Reiki, or that they don't want to be initiated, because it won't be a learning experience. But know this, believe that you need to learn everything on your own is false, and true at the same time.. Because you're never alone, there are people here, who can help you get this "flash" first, so you can learn things later. Reiki initiation and general Reiki practice is such flash you get the seed, and you can watch it grow as you like it. Reiki is very individual practice you start it with teacher's help, but everything else is your own, personal Reiki gnosis. The more people receive Reiki, the better this world will be.

How Stress Affects Your Body, From Your Brain to Your Digestive System

It's one thing to feel occasional stress. But when you're constantly under pressure and have no way to cope, your risk of developing serious illness climbs. Here's what you need to know about the long-term effects of living a stressed-out life.If you've ever felt stressed out (and who hasn't?), you already know that being under pressure can affect your body, either by causing a headache, muscle tightness, or flutters in your chest; making you feel down in the dumps; or leaving you ravenous for chocolate or robbed of all appetite.

But these stress symptoms are merely the signals of the deeper impact that chronic stress can have on every organ and system in your body, from your nervous and circulatory systems to your digestive and immune systems.

The Good News About Stress
Not all stress is bad, and the hormones that the body produces in response to stress aren't, either. Their levels actually fluctuate throughout the day as you adapt to challenges such as waking up (yes, that's an example of stress), getting stuck in traffic, or being surprised for your birthday.

It's also possible to manage stress by doing small things like deep breathing, taking a walk, listening to a meditation app, or even grabbing your child's fidget spinner to distract yourself from whatever's stressing you out. Any of these strategies can help short-circuit the body's fight-or-flight response, stopping the flood of stress hormones from revving up your blood pressure and heart rate

**Even Short-Term Stress Can Affect Your Body,
Especially Your Heart**
When you're stressed, your heart rate goes up and so does your blood pressure. Most people can handle these

kinds of physiological changes in stride. Cortisol is released when you feel stressed, but the level of this hormone should go back down when the stressful event is over. Even short-term stress can have a profound impact on your heart if it's bad enough. The condition cardiomyopathy, also known as broken-heart syndrome, is a weakening of the heart's left ventricle (its main pumping chamber) that usually results from severe emotional or physical stress.

Although the condition is in general rare, 90 percent of cases are in women.

Cardiomyopathy can occur in very stressful situations, such as after a huge fight, the death of a child, or other major triggers. Patients come into the emergency room with severe chest pain and other symptoms of what we call acute heart failure syndrome, though their coronary arteries are clear. They can be very sick, but with treatment, most of the time, people recover.

Should I Get a Stress Test

A stress test doesn't measure the stress in your life, but it does measure the stress on your heart, or rather how hard your heart is working and what it looks like when you're walking very fast on a steep incline on a treadmill. People usually get a stress test when they have multiple risk factors for heart disease, or if they've been having certain symptoms like chest pain or palpitations. Basically, we want to see what happens to the heart when there is a greater demand for oxygen: when the blood pressure and blood flow increase. That's when you can see if there might be an obstruction that is blocking blood flow in the arteries that needs treatment.

Why Long-Term Stress Is So Bad for Your Body Systems

Left unchecked, severe stress, the kind that continues for months or years is more apt to lead to serious illness than short-term stressors do.

The stress hormones cortisol, adrenaline, and epinephrine affect most areas of the body, interfering with sleep and increasing the risk of stroke, high blood pressure, and heart disease, as well as causing depression and anxiety. Here are a few key ways chronic stress can impact the body:

Stress causes inflammation.
Studies have shown that chronic stress is linked to increased inflammation in the body. One of the proposed actions of stress is that it triggers inflammation in the body, which is thought to underlie many diseases, including heart disease, diabetes, autoimmune disorders like multiple sclerosis, and even pain.

One possible culprit: Chronic stress seems to be linked to an increase in pro-inflammatory cytokines, a type of immune cell that is typically part of the body's defense system when you have an infection.

People with autoimmune conditions, where the immune system attacks the body itself, tend to have higher levels of these cytokines. The good news is that stress management techniques such as meditation have been shown to have anti-inflammatory effects, lowering cytokines in the body.

Stress affects your digestive tract.
The gastrointestinal tract is filled with nerve endings and immune cells, all of which are affected by stress hormones. As a result, stress can cause acid reflux as well as exacerbate symptoms of irritable bowel syndrome and inflammatory bowel disease. Not to mention create butterflies in your stomach.

Stress messes with your immune system.
A number of studies shows that stress lowers immunity, which may be why you're likely to come down with a cold after a crunch time at school or work right on the first day of your vacation. Patients with autoimmune disorders often say they get flare-ups during or after stressful events, or tell me that their condition began after a particularly stressful event.

Stress can muddle your brain.
Brain scans of people with post-traumatic stress disorder show more activity in the amygdala, a brain region associated with fear and emotion. But even everyday kinds of stress can affect how the brain processes information.

We see actual structural, functional, and connectivity-related brain changes in people who are under chronic stress. All of these can affect cognition and attention, which is why you may find it hard to focus or learn new things when you are stressed.

Stress can make you feel crummy all over. Stress makes us more sensitive to pain, and it can also cause pain due to muscular tension. People under stress also tend to perceive pain differently.

They're also less apt to sleep well, which doesn't help matters. Sleep is so important in terms of helping to prevent every disease. It helps reboot the immune system and prevents depression, irritability, and exhaustion.

Getting Cancer From Stress or to Die From It
While it's tough to link stress directly to a specific disease, we know that stress does contribute to serious illness. Forty percent of cancers are preventable with changes in lifestyle. Since stress makes you more likely to smoke, drink excessively, and eat in ways that cause

obesity, it's fair to say that there is a link between stress and disease.

Maybe it's no accident that most heart attacks occur on Monday the most stressful day of the week.

Reiki, Energy Therapy for Multiple Sclerosis
Like acupuncture, tai chi, and qigong, Reiki which means "universal life force energy" aims to alter the flow of energy in and around the body, and is believed to facilitate relaxation, improve sleep, reduce anxiety and fatigue, and, perhaps, address more specific symptoms such as pain and spasticity.

The ability to perform Reiki is transferred from a master to a student in a process known as an attunement.

How Is Reiki Done for MS
Reiki treatments, which typically last 45 to 60 minutes, "are administered through the healing hands of a certified practitioner with the client lying fully clothed on a massage table. There's no manipulation of bones or tissues. The practitioner merely holds her hands on,

above, or around the client's body to channel energy. Some clients, will fall asleep during a session, and most report a sense of "warmth, peace, and relaxation."

Reiki, can also be sent distantly, as it is an energy and therefore is not bound to one geographic location. In addition, patients can become attuned so they can provide Reiki therapy to themselves, and caregivers can also learn to practice.

Are Reiki's Effects on MS Real
Although little scientific research has been completed on Reiki, there are many patients and practitioners who believe in its benefits. Despite the lack of evidence and even in light of conflicting study results, Reiki is in great demand and is practiced by nurses and others at hundreds of hospitals and health centers across the country. It's offered at renowned hospitals such as the Memorial Sloan Kettering Cancer Center in New York City, and the Dana-Farber Cancer Institute in Boston, and is a service provided at the Multiple Sclerosis Center at Rhode Island Hospital in Providence.

Whether or not Reiki's benefits are the result of a placebo effect, as some suggest, it's popular because patients claim it works. It can greatly benefit anyone who suffers from a chronic or an acute illness. Reiki helps reduce stress and anxiety, balancing the body's energy system to allow for healing while helping the body heal itself.

In a review published in the Journal of Evidence-Based Complementary & Alternative Medicine in 2017, Reiki was found to be more effective than placebo (sham Reiki) or progressive muscle relaxation in reducing pain, depression, and anxiety in chronically ill individuals.

The review included 13 studies and concluded that the studies provided reasonably strong support for Reiki being more effective than placebo, and that the practice is a safe and gentle 'complementary' therapy that activates the parasympathetic nervous system to heal body and mind.

Common Benefits for People With MS

Sometimes clients don't feel anything immediately after a Reiki session, but benefits may be seen in as little as one session, depending on what the client needs and desires. Many people report a sense of calm, decreased stress, and improved rest following even one session.

Reiki, being the highest form of energy, goes where it is needed to promote healing and, therefore, works on every level, including physical, mental, and spiritual. It also may be used to address particular symptoms, with practitioners setting an intention for it to heal in those particular areas. However, Reiki always knows what healing is needed, and so we trust in that process.

Even Reiki Skeptics Can Feel Its Effects

Such comments may raise eyebrows and provoke disbelief, even ridicule. But it's not necessary for a person to believe in Reiki for it to work. Try it and then talk to mute. I've had many skeptics walk through my door and leave an hour later totally in awe of how they are feeling.

Reiki is not a cure for MS. I don't believe it's a quick fix or a miraculous healing technique. However, the energy is known to bring balance to one's physical, emotional, and spiritual needs.

Four Levels of Reiki Attunement

Anyone can be attuned to perform Reiki. We aren't changing the energy. The four levels of training as being increasingly advanced and working with progressively higher levels of energy.

Level 1 is generally for people who are just learning and is mostly used for self-Reiki and for friends and family. Level 2 teaches how to send Reiki distantly and incorporates Reiki on a more emotional level. Level 3 incorporates Reiki on a more spiritual plane, and students learn more advanced techniques.

The final level leads to the ability to practice as a Reiki master teacher, teaching Reiki and giving attunements.

Lisa took a Reiki level 1 attunement. For the first 21 days and afterward I practiced daily as recommended. I followed a series of hand positions every evening and found it to be meditative and relaxing, and I would shortly fall into a deep and restful sleep.

I would absolutely recommend anybody to try it, not only MS patients. There is no downside. Relaxation and restful sleep in itself is healing for the body. To have another available tool for relaxation is wonderful.

Negative Intentions in the Practice of Reiki
Because Reiki is an intelligent energy and it knows what must be healed, and how it must be healed, we as practitioners must learn few things about intentions, with which we channel this spiritual energy. An intention is "what we want" I want something, so I have a specific intention – to own something, achieve something, learn something. In Reiki, the intention is "that" what we want for ourselves or another person when it comes to results of healing.

In different methods of spiritual healing, people, like psychic healers, create entire programs (sets) of intentions. They control the energy, so they take care of nearly everything during healing. In Reiki, we're not really in control of the energy we just channel it. Our intentions are limited. During the Reiki treatment, we can intend the following:

1. The primary, honest intention is that we ask Reiki to heal the person in accordance with the highest good; also, we ask Reiki to help the person achieve the state of balance, harmony and health.

2. The second intention is that we can ask Reiki to heal a specific problem – for example, a headache or specific illness or emotional issue, or to be more detailed, the source and cause of this particular health or emotional issue.

3. We merge these intentions together – when we begin the treatment, we ask for Reiki, we open the energy flow, so the energy can be channeled. While doing so, we can say in our mind:

I ask Reiki to heal the source of this person's headache and act in accordance with the highest good of this person, and with the highest good of all living beings.

This is related to one of the Five Principles of Reiki that is often translated as "respect all living beings". With this intention, we direct energy to a specific issue, but we allow it to heal the source of the problem. Reiki knows what must be healed. You don't have to know what is the source of the problem especially if a lot of illness can be merely symptoms of a deeper problem. But Reiki knows it, and it will act accordingly.

What's more, our intentions need to be honest you really need to intend to heal the person. Wishing to perform a treatment session in order to charge money is not enough. If you do not have honest intentions, you cannot perform the treatment. Such dishonest intentions happen, and it's normal. We might feel anger towards the person, or sexual arousal; or negative emotions, for example, if the person is gay, and we do not tolerate gays. When you feel similar emotions, this leads to dishonest intentions, and the treatment cannot be successful and honest. This is the time when the intentions must be healed. Thus, don't worry if you have these unpleasant intentions – it's natural for most people. But it also means that becoming aware of these intentions is a perfect opportunity to do some healing work upon you.

It's application of the rule: "first, heal yourself" and you have many tools to do so, starting with Five Principles through meditations to self-treatment sessions. For example, if you feel angry towards the person, you may begin self-treatment sessions with the intention of healing this anger and acting in agreement with the highest good of you and the person in question.

Generally, it's the best thing to do whenever you have a problem of either physical or emotional nature, and you don't know what to do, send yourself Reiki in a form of regular self-treatment sessions. Reiki will guide you and soon you will learn how to solve and heal the issues. By completing the first degree class, you receive a powerful tool that can heal everything if you only allow it to.

If you feel that your previous intentions and unpleasant emotions are healed, you can treat the person that you were unable to treat in the past. Remember, as Reiki practitioner you honestly have to wish the other person recovery, happiness, peace and harmony because, as practitioners, this is what we promote through our life and work.

I often explain the way Reiki heals through a metaphor of stairs. Imagine simple wooden stairs by doing self-treatment on a regular basis, working with the Five Principles and by healing yourself, you walk onto the first step on the stairs in question. Then, you are capable of healing all people who stand on the very same step. But a lot of people stands on steps above the one you're standing on. Thus, you cannot heal them as their problems are beyond your reach. You have to continue healing yourself, so after few weeks, you can progress, and stand on the second step. Then, you will be able to heal people from that step, and the step below it. The more you work on yourself, the higher you are on these spiritual stairs and the more people you can actually heal, because, in some way, you have done your homework, you have healed all the things from the steps you have conquered, and because you know these problems yourself, you can heal these problems in others.

Thus, you won't be able to heal everyone at once some people will be far beyond your reach, but there will be others, people you can truly help. By keeping the intention of honest healing in your mind, you attract people that you can heal for real, and not simple for money.

All of the above is the basic aspect of intentions in Reiki, but there is more negative intentions are part of the healing process, and even if painful, this subject must be discussed in details. We do this because this knowledge is very important for safe and effective practice of Reiki.

Negative Intentions While Working With Reiki
Reiki itself is a powerful healing method which can do no harm yet it is not always the case, since sometimes, in our practice, we might not send Reiki, but our own bioenergy and as such, our own bioenergy contains our emotions and different sort of "programs" beliefs, fears or even manipulative thoughts. In order to send Reiki, whole Reiki and only Reiki, you as a practitioner should work on healing your intentions in order words, you

need to heal the way you subconsciously think about people you're trying to help.

Sometimes, your intention might be hidden within your subconscious mind, and even if you think you're helping the person, your lower-self, your subconscious mind, is doing the opposite. Take a look at another example.

Let's say your brother asks you for Reiki healing you agree, even if you know that you're in conflict with your brother, and for some time now, you had bad thoughts about him (like wishing him some bad stuff). Even if you pretend to have positive intentions about your brother, and even if you believe that your intentions are clear because you might honestly wish to heal your relationship with your brother unconsciously you might have the opposite intentions. Your lower-self, your subconscious mind, might act according to the stored programs and beliefs and it will block your efforts to channel Reiki. Instead, it will send your own bioenergy with your programs and negative energies of aggression or even hate, or at least dislike.

Even if Reiki initiations supports us in this case making sure that whenever we intend to send Reiki, we do send Reiki, sometimes and I mean it, sometimes things go wrong, and instead of Reiki, we send our own bioenergy, which might carry negative programs to another person, and we might not be conscious of it. You might not be aware of this, but it might happen.

In the example above, the negative beliefs and mind patterns about the "brother" caused by bad experiences, and conflicts from the past created a subconscious negative intention that is far more important for energy work than your conscious mind. It's because your subconscious mind governs the energy channels and centers, through which Reiki energy flows – and if your subconscious mind is ruled by emotions of hate and aggression, then it might close the channels to Reiki, and send bioenergy because it falsely believes that it's the best thing to do.

Consciously, you might wish the person all the best but subconsciously, due to past events, you might have negative thoughts, and thus, negative intentions you're not truly in control of these, but you're responsible for healing them but we'll deal with this in just few minutes. There are two additional cases of bad intentions.

Let's say you're a heterosexual male, and there's a sexy, young 19 years old girl lying on the massage table, waiting for you to give her a Reiki healing session how do you react, hmm? I gave this example intentionally because it's a normal, healthy and genetically-based reaction to experience sexual excitement. Now, if this would be your girlfriend, or wife, then sexual attraction is normal. But it's not normal if you're about to give the other person a Reiki healing session. In such case, your intention should be to heal the person without any sexual thoughts. But when you approach the girl with sexual thoughts (because you want to touch her) and without any intention of true healing, then this is a really bad intention which will block Reiki flow, and let's say it, it will be an unethical sexual abuse.

Finally, there's a type of clearly bad intention:

There's a person visiting a Reiki healer, a person that is interested in Reiki course. But the teacher, instead of initiating into Reiki practice, plugs the person into his own energetic net of donors, to drain their energy for his own benefits, and in addition, the teacher programs the person that she will never free herself from this particular teacher this is a very negative thing to do. From a healing session perspective, when a person visits such practitioner, he is programing a new thought in the person's mind, that this person will never go to other healers and that she will constantly return to this particular Reiki practitioner for more "healing". Both such examples clearly shows a negative intention a will of the practitioner to do harm.

Therefore, even if Reiki cannot do harm, the practitioner can. With all the examples above I've met in my Reiki practice some of come from my personal experience, some of them were passed to me by my Reiki friends. And since there are many of such negative intentions that we store in our mind, it's our duty as Reiki practitioners to identify these intentions, and to heal them, so we can become better healers.

The link between your health and happiness
Happiness means different things to different people. For some, it could mean spending time with loved ones, for others it would be travelling solo, for some it could involve pursuing a hobby. Whatever rates high on your 'happiness index' deserves to be an important part of your life, say experts. This recommendation comes after an increasing number of studies have revealed that health has a lot to do with your happiness levels.

While there are lots of self-help and feel-good books available and apps that encourage you to focus on the positive aspects of life, a lot depends on your own mindset. So, make an effort to focus on the good things in life, even if you can't think of a lot of points. Once you figure out (and readily accept) things that bring you joy, your mind will automatically begin to look at life in a different way. And this, reckon experts, will eventually have a positive impact on your health. Here are health benefits that happiness can bring.

It helps you fight stress

Stress is inevitable in today's day and time. No matter what you do or where you live, tension can be inescapable and affect you mentally as well as physically. And stress in the long run can lead to a host of serious ailments. While happiness won't keep stress completely at bay, it will help you cope with it better. Happy people seem to have lower levels of cortisol a hormone associated with stress and this helps them deal with stressful situations and emotions in a far better way than their tension-ridden counterparts.

It's good for your heart

As cheesy as this might sound, it holds true. Happy people are said to have better blood pressure levels and heart rates. In fact, certain studies even go a step further and say that people who are happier reportedly have superior heart rate variability. This refers to the interval between heartbeats, which is important for good heart health. Over years, this will lower your chances of suffering from coronary heart disease.

It helps your body deal with pain better
Your state of mind not only helps you when it comes to your emotional health but also has a big role to play in your physical well-being. Researchers say that people who are happy and positive seem to suffer less from cough and cold, heartburn, indigestion, body ache or painful joints, for example. This is because, when there is a general feeling of satisfaction and a sense of gratitude, you are able to deal with physical pain better.

It's connected with longevity
Happiness is a choice that you have to make don't leave this option in someone else's hands. While making this a part of life takes patience and practice, once you train your mind to be happy, it will become a habit. And a good one, too. A number of studies have revealed that happiness and longevity are related. When you regularly experience feelings of fulfilment, delight and affection, it seems to add years to your life.

It boosts your immune system

How many times have you heard that your immunity has a lot to do with how often you fall sick? Well, here's something to add to it. You can now give a much-needed boost to your immune system by choosing to be happy. Researchers say that sullen and testy people tend to fall ill more often. This, they say, has a lot to do with how your body reacts to emotions the happier you are, the better your body fights off infections.

Health benefits

According to practitioners, the healing effects are mediated by channeling the universal energy known as qi, pronounced "chi." In India, this is known as "prana." This is the same energy involved in tai chi exercise. It is the life force energy that some believe surrounds all of us.

This energy is said to permeate the body. Reiki experts point out that, while this energy is not measurable by modern scientific techniques, it can be felt by many who tune in to it. Reiki is alleged to aid relaxation, assist in the body's natural healing processes, and develop emotional, mental, and spiritual well-being.

It is also said to induce deep relaxation, help people cope with difficulties, relieve emotional stress, and improve overall wellbeing.

People who receive Reiki describe it as "intensely relaxing."

Conditions that Reiki has been used to help treat include:

- cancer
- heart disease
- anxiety
- depression
- chronic pain
- infertility
- neurodegenerative disorders
- autism
- Crohn's disease
- fatigue syndromes

According to the University of Minnesota, patients who have undergone a Reiki session may say:

- "I feel very refreshed and seem to be thinking more clearly."
- "I think I fell asleep."
- "I can't believe how hot your hands got!"
- "I feel more relaxed than even after a massage."
- "My headache is gone."

Cancer patients who have Reiki say they feel better after. This may be because it helps them relax. Another reason, according to Cancer Research U.K. could be that the therapist spends time with them and touches them. This has a soothing effect on patients who may be overwhelmed by invasive therapy, fear, and stress.

Individuals report different experiences. Some say that the practitioner's hands become hot, others report cooling hands and some people feel pulsating waves. The most common reports are of a release of stress and deep relaxation.

Reiki's healing power: What is the evidence

While Reiki grows in popularity, questions remain. Reiki claims to enable relaxation, reduce pain, speed healing, and improve some symptoms, but few research findings support any specific health benefits. It has been criticized for claiming to heal diseases without scientific evidence. Some have described its claims as fraudulent.

Critics say that it flies in the face of our current understanding of the laws of nature. Advocates respond that the benefits of wellbeing and reduced stress are real but hard to measure with a scientific study.

Scientists note that high-quality research into its effectiveness is lacking. No study has yet shown that it is any more effective than a placebo, they say.

A literature review published in 2008 concluded that there was not enough evidence to support Reiki as an effective treatment for any condition, and that its value remained unproven.

A review of studies on Reiki and the treatment of anxiety and depression was published by Cochrane. The investigators concluded that there was "insufficient evidence to say whether or not Reiki is useful for people over 16 years of age with anxiety or depression or both." Of the few studies that had been done, most were of a low quality, with small sample sizes, no peer review, or no control group.

Meanwhile, research published in BMC Nephrology has suggested that allowing dialysis patients, for example, to benefit from the "healing touch" may be worthwhile, especially if it offered for free by volunteers. Pain reduction may be only slight, but it is non-traumatic, does no harm, and allows patients to feel they are "doing something" themselves to ease their pain.

More recently, Annie Harrington told MNT that the U.K. Reiki Federation currently has a "large document cataloging many research trials." Maybe these findings, which are being studied by the Federation and the U.K.'s Complementary and Natural Healthcare Council (CNHC), will help bring Reiki further into the mainstream.

Regulatory issues: Time for a change

Regulatory authorities sometimes ask Reiki websites to change their information to conform with legal standards. Sites selling Reiki products may carry a legal disclaimer, stating that the products are not a medical device, and not intended for use in diagnosing, healing, or preventing disease.

In the U.K., the Advertising Standards Agency (ASA) has rejected claims that Reiki can heal a range of diseases on a number of occasions.

Judy Kosovich, in a study published by Physics Procedia, calls for a "fresh look" at the regulation of energy medicine. While accepting that regulatory bodies exist to protect the public, she argues that there is still much about how the body works that is not understood or described by science.

Is Reiki harmful

The U.S. National Center for Complementary and Integrative Health (NCCIH) state that Reiki "has not been clearly shown to be useful for any health-related purpose." However, they add that it does not appear to have any harmful effects.

The main concern appears to be that people with serious health issues may opt for Reiki and other complementary therapies instead of rigorously tested modern medicine. However, using it alongside other treatments is unlikely to be hazardous.

Indeed, touch alone, whether with or without "universal energy," appears to have a range of benefits, from building trust to enhancing overall wellbeing.

Expensive conventional treatments that are currently available often have serious adverse effects, and may or may not work. Many people, therefore, would like the freedom to choose an alternative.

Conclusion

During a meditation several years after developing Reiki, Mikao Usui decided to add the Reiki Ideals to the practice of Reiki. The Ideals came in part from the five prinicples of the Meiji emperor of Japan whom Mikao Usui admired. The Ideals were developed to add spiritual balance to Usui Reiki. Their purpose is to help people realize that healing the spirit by consciously deciding to improve oneself is a necessary part of the Reiki healing experience. In order for the Reiki healing energies to have lasting results, the client must accept responsibility for her or his healing and take an active part in it. Therefore, the Usui system of Reiki is more than the use of the Reiki energy. It must also include an active commitment to improve oneself in order for it to be a complete system. The ideals are both guidelines for living a gracious life and virtues worthy of practice for their inherent value.

Reiki has had a positive affect on all forms of illness and negative conditions. This includes minor things like head or stomach aches, bee stings, colds, flu, tension and anxiety as well as serious illness like heart disease, cancer, leukemia, etc. The side effects of regular medical treatments have also been reduced or eliminated. This includes the negative effects of chemotherapy, post operative pain and depression as well as improving the healing rate and reducing the time needed to stay in the hospital. Reiki always helps and in some cases people have experienced complete healings which have been confirmed by medical tests before and after the Reiki treatments. However, while some have experienced miracles, they cannot be guaranteed. Stress reduction with some improvement in ones physical and psychological condition are what most experience.

This is one of the wonderful benefits of Reiki and is why it is such a wonderful technique for the new millennium. It allows individuals and groups to do something positive about the challenging situations we see on the news involving so many people all over the planet. Reiki can be used to reduce suffering and help people any where in the world. See our World Peace Grid Project. As more and more people send Reiki to help the world heal, we will move quickly to a world of peace and harmony.

www.ingramcontent.com/pod-product-compliance
Lightning Source LLC
Chambersburg PA
CBHW060942130726
48001CB00003B/1025